Made in the USA
Middletown, DE
25 October 2022

13478047R00057